America is a tune. It must be sung together.
-Gerald Stanley Lee, Crowds

We can't all be Washingtons, but we can all be patriots.
-Charles F. Browne

VOTOPHICS BOOKS

Published by Votophics Media

a subsidiary of Gold Ribbons Group

Republic of Biafra

+234-706-8435-789

First published on amazon kindle direct publishing

A self publishing tool

ISBN 978-1521793732

Printed in US, UK, and others.

TRUMP EFFECT

AMERICA'S DOOM OR BOOM?

P. A. HAS

TRUMP EFFECT:

AMERICA'S DOOM OR BOOM?

BY

P. A. HAS

VOTOPHICS BOOKS

DEDICATION

This book is dedicated to all Americans who have remained true to their country. And to my pretty, Mercy Shols, for her kind support.

INTRODUCTORY NOTE

Trump Effect: America's Doom or Boom?

THE EMERGENCE OF DONALD TRUMP on America's political scene and his subsequent rise to power is a huge shocker to the mainstream politicians. It was unprecedented; something the establishment had thought is absolutely impossible, and more unlikely to happen. They were completely taken unawares. Even his opponents are yet to grasp the extent to which his victory has swept through the American political landscape. The reverberations it sent across the world is still boggling the mind of great proponents of globalization, people who had thought his views on the subject would cause his defeat.

The ripple effect is far beyond American borders, touching even the remote places in Africa, a continent of dependents. It has given many a cause to worry about the future of the global order of the world. Equally, it has put smile on the faces of a thousand more nationalists who see his emergence as a gift for the salvation of the world from the throes of the liberal taunted globalization.

In spite of the daily dolling out of biased polls by the mainstream media in US and the entire western world, Trump's fame and sphere of influence have continued to widen. His effect on the current world political stake has not shown any sign of cessation. The recent reception in Poland is a huge shocker to his detractors. This daily increase in followership on social media is something the detractors do not want to point out.

Some people might want to claim that this effect will only put a big deficit on the position of America's relationship with the rest of the world in the global political stage, yet his supporters have refused to accept anything other than that his is a daring stand up to the corrupt self centred elites who seemed determined to sift the world of the common man and turn the world into a paradise for the gloriously wealthy few. He is seen as a dissident elitist insider revolting against his class in favour of the neglected class of the masses. For me, he is the repairer of the breach. Like a messiah sent to bring America and the west back to the path of national satisfaction and protection of sovereign states as against the modern day imperialism in the name of global intervention on national affairs without the consultation of the will and choice of the people.

His emergence is not just for the good of America, it also puts an end to the meddlesomeness of the previous liberal controlled Washington in world affairs: the removal of regimes and legitimately elected leaders of the third world country whose vision for their country does not align with the global imperialistic order. This had, for the past eight years, left US an apologetic nation, instead of the big brother role it is supposed to be playing in order to ensure peace, stability and equity in all parts of the world.

Trump effect has equally exposed the weaknesses of the American democratic setting, their intelligence community, the mainstream media and America's liberal society, the worst in the world so far in my opinion. It has shown how hypocritical the American democracy has become in recent years, how uncertain and compromised American spy agencies can be about major incidences, how biased the liberal owned mainstream media is as well as how desperate and intolerant American liberal society can get while angling for their egocentric, unaccommodating political views. It has also raised the question on the migration leakages in western countries through the Islamization tool of world refugee intake by the developed countries.

Does this effect mean doom or boom for America and its people? What will happen if the current trend of divisiveness it has exposed is not curbed? Does Donald Trump have the will to upturn every established policy that negates the will of majority of Americans and the world? This and more are discussed in the following articles.

I want to also make it clear here that no aspect of this book was contrived, but are merely built upon my personal opinions having observed world affairs since the emergence of Trump on the American political scene.

Added Definition: *Trump Effect is a form of unprecedented political change taking place in a society to help realign it to pursuing the collective interest of the populace instead of the interest of the selected few global minded bureaucrats. It exposes underlying divisiveness in the society not previously pronounced.*

ARTICLE ONE

My Letter to President Donald Trump

Sir,

First, I want to specially congratulate you on the big victory you witnessed at the last presidential poll, winning both the electoral votes, which are far more important, and the popular vote, not regarding the illegal votes cast for your key opponent in those big elitist cities. Though it was not very easy, but through your untiring efforts in reaching every neglected part of America with your campaign rallies, places where your opponent did not deem necessary to visit in person, you nailed the US presidency. You so finely carried the message of hope for America's return to glory that even the skeptics before the election, could not put you down with their harsh rhetoric and negative predictions.

American's loved your strength, and wanted you for their president not minding you were called a political novice who was said to lack both the experience and competence needed to run the country's highest office. It is true I did not vote for you because am not an American citizen neither do I live in the US, but I knew all along then that you were going to emerge a winner, despite the negative reports in the media – talks about not been able to beat your supposedly more experienced and mainstream supported opponent who appeared to be more politically correct in her demeanor. I knew this by merely following the responses and reactions of the American citizenry to events and arguments during the campaign trail on social media and mainstream media!

I believe you will not disappoint the confidence the US electorate had and still have in you. However, you must ignore your detractors in the media, the losing Democrats and a couple of aggrieved people in your party who seem uncomfortable with the people's decision to make you their president. I do not understand why these bodies still drive their futile un-American quests, knowing they have only always failed since your emergence in the political scene.

Their refusal to accept your victory should not bother you in any way. They thought you would not win in the polls, but were disappointed to the point of shedding tears on that election night. They fought to turn the Electoral College votes against you, but ended up losing more of their own electoral vote than you did yours. They thought they could use their cries of vote of no confidence to dissuade the congress from confirming your victory, but it turned out they were the ones losing more seats in congress. Turning their attention to the swing states with claims of manipulation of the vote counts, they sought to deny you of the resounding win you got In those states. Sadly, they lost more of the votes previously accrued to their candidate.

They came with the Russian story in full force even before your inauguration, but have unsurprisingly been unable to convince the American masses that they are not on a political witch hunt against your government. They even tried to take the congress seats you left vacant with your appointment of secretaries of departments; they lost all, including a run-off election in one place. You see, you have every reason to decide to treat them with complete disdain, especially as it is evident that the hand of God under whose guide the American union was constituted is behind your coming to power. With that, you have less need of those who have sworn to fight instead of work with your new government. Ignoring them in most cases is important if you don't want to have them keep you from solving the problems Americans elected you to solve. Even so, trying to answer to every unnecessary question they raise might lead to the possibility of making a colossal mistake on your part.

You must focus on keeping all the promises for which you were given the mandate. In doing that, there is need for thorough and deliberate effort to bring the interest of every American to bear in major policies and reforms, be it in health, taxes, immigration or infrastructural development. Though some of the more liberal populace may not grasp the need for your changes now, make it something that will turn out eventually for the good of every one. Nothing should be done in haste. Consultations are needed, and should be as bipartisan as can be readily provided. These will help make your administration successful in the long run.

I also believe the Americans who put you in that office like the way you use social media to speak to them. I particularly see it as more accurate than what the media dishes out. However, you must not give them any reason to discredit those who work with you. Inasmuch as I have not seen any contradictions as the media hypes it to be, it is still useful that you ask those who speak for you to keep quiet on any subject they do not know exactly what you think about them in the moment they are facing the press. This will help silence the fake reporting in the media. We all know that the basic tenets of unbiased reporting in journalism no longer exist in major American media outlets. They have chosen to be political instead of being neutral/ apolitical. You need to treat them with as much disregard as your country's constitution allows.

Specifically, ignore the reports they are busy releasing in batches to discredit your administration. They are nothing to the patriotic Americans, hence you need not make any effort to defend or excuse yourself, let your legal team handle those irrelevant stories. Do not let them make you lose focus from your agenda.

Also, if the media refuse to talk about the many positive things and successes your team is recording, do not get bothered. Put them up in the social media for us to see. Who even spends more time in front of the TV screen than they do in front of their phones and PC screens? We barely even notice these media neglects. Who cares? Besides, these successes are being witnessed by the American people, and they know about them. Those not visible in clear sense can be explained out.

Very importantly, I want to advice you on how to handle the Russian stories being peddled by the opposition media. Treat them as bluffs, with silence most of the times. And try to fully support the instituted investigations going on as that is the only way it can all be put to rest eventually, particularly that of the special council. You have nothing to be worried about in doing that; your supporters will love you to do this. Besides, with the way the story is going, it is more likely to backfire in the face of those peddling it. I do not know if they realize this, but they have broken American laws in their effort to discredit your election. You can ask for a broader look into this Russian story and how it has built up so far to this day, with focus on both sides of the divide; who does not want to know about the incriminating information on Clinton that was supposedly promised your campaign.

There is one thing obvious in the Russian story: it's turning up much more like a false narrative, a political set up or attempt at overshadowing the real criminal activities of the opposition. It remains so unless proven otherwise with substantial evidence. I believe the Russians are not US chief political adversary as been propagated in America today. I also strongly believe that a large set of bureaucrats who connived with China companies to steal American jobs because of the cheap labour they get over there are using the Russian story to distract the government. You should try and look into this. Find out how much money is coming to the US political fund raising from China, and possibly Russia. You might be shocked to realize why everyone in the establishment seems to want the

Russian people and their government tagged as enemy to the US. There have so far been no concrete evidence that pins Russian government to these allegations, but speculations, except there are ones we do not know about that can serve as evidence, which I suppose you are privy to, in the form of classified information. If there are, fighting Russians, even in the coldest way possible, is not the best solution. This is merely my opinion though.

I see Russians to be mere scapegoats, blackmailed for their Soviet-linked past, but I suppose they are not America's enemy more than China is! Their government seriously wants a reset in the relationship between both countries. Work to achieve that, as I strongly believe it will serve America's interest in the long run. Partner with them where necessary, but never ever appear to go to war with them, in reality or in rhetoric. They may not be as powerful as America is, but they, like a strong small boy standing up to a big boy bully, wants to hold their own grounds and front their own powers. It is better to work with Russia than with any other country in the world in ensuring that peace reigns around the world, especially in the fight against terrorism. Every form of imperialism must be made to completely cease from our globe. Countries should be independent of others as much as possible, except in bilateral agreements.

In the fight against terrorism and radical Islamic extremism, countries must be free to choose to protect their borders from being infiltrated by hoodlums who might camouflage as refugees and immigrants. Your travel ban is a good move. However, the easiest way to defeat the terrorists from this world is to make religious leaders and communities around the world, especially in the east, account for every individual walking their streets and sitting in their halls of worship. This will make it easier to know the activities of individuals who might be linked to terrorist organizations. And in fighting these criminals, it is better to work with the local forces in countries where these organizations exist. The recent victory in Mosul, Iraq is an example of how successful this method can be. Maintaining peace after such victories is equally very important.

When it comes to dictatorial regimes in any country of the world, outside governments have no right to interfere in other countries method of governance, not withstanding where UN might be standing on this. However, diplomatic measures can be used to make such governments either get better or let their own people choose through a peaceful means what they want for their country. World powers, especially your country, should cease from supporting armed militants against sitting foreign governments. There are other ways to resolve such issues than promoting suffering and death in the guise of assisting in the fight for freedom of any people. What happened in Syria after the use of the chemical power by the Assad regime is the surest way to prevent the use of military power against individuals fighting for any sort of freedom.

The US can convince the United Nations on how best to ensure that people's voices are heard and implemented in their own country, and not the imposition of any outside government, super power or not.

With that, I want to call on your government to come to the rescue of my people, the Biafrans, who have been marginalized from the day this country, Nigeria, was given independence. Our fathers in the early years of the country's independence sought to correct this anomaly, especially with the Aburi accord agreements which the then Nigerian government botched. As a result, our fathers fought a war in which the Nigerian government with outside supports committed one of the worst genocides in the history of mankind. No one has been questioned for those senseless massacres of innocent Biafrans, particularly those of the Igbo decent. More so, we are not even asking for that to be visited. In the least, not yet. Instead, we are crying out to the US and the UN to help us get free from these shackles of political and economic subjugation of a people who also happen to be the mainstay of the entire Nigerian nation.

We do not want to remain a part of this failing nation. Some self-centred fellows who claim to be speaking for the Biafran people and are parading themselves as our leaders were not sent by us. Their call for a unified and more inclusive Nigeria has fallen on deaf ears for the past 50 years since the Biafran war. They are still trying to use same call for unity to distract from what the people of Biafra truly want. The Biafran people do not want to continue with this alliance. We have no confidence in the future of the alliance; neither do we want to keep waiting for things to get better. We do not want restructuring in any form they are brandishing it; they brandished it even before the war and still abdicated from implementing the solutions in then accord which led to that gruesome war. Over the years of their rule and intimidation of the Biafrans, they have continued to embezzle public funds in the guise of national dialogues, but they keep throwing the resolutions to the trash can of national archives. We do not want this anymore. We are fed up. We want our own country with territorial entity and right, and we will keep fighting till we get it!

It is even very clear today that our lives are in jeopardy in the Nigerian nation with threats to drive our people from their places of business and dwellings in the core Nigerian territories. We fear for the safety of our people in those areas. The government of Nigeria, apart from mere talks and empty promises has not done anything, nor are prepared to do anything to safeguard the lives of our people in their country. We ask for US and UN intervention in that situation before another genocide on Biafrans, though we are not handicapped ourselves should any stupid things be done against our people.

We are not asking for war; we are not even killing or shooting any guns, not that we do not have the capability or will to do so and prevail at it in resistance to the constant killing of our people, but we understand the importance of freedom through dialogue. We are asking for this dialogue to ONLY begin with the conduct of a referendum in Biafran land. Britain had such chances, Turkey too. The people in those countries had to choose what they want for themselves. What different are we from those that we cannot have one for us here in Biafran land. We are fully prepared to come to the table with whatever becomes the outcome of that referendum when it is done and we are prepared to implement whatever the people decide. We want peace and not war. The Nigerian government keeps going back to the history of war against our secessionist fathers some of which are no longer alive today. The agitation for Biafra today, in my opinion, is not a secessionist one anymore. Biafra is already a nation. We are only calling to be left to formally withdraw from this union with the north and west that has not worked since inception. This call is our unmitigated and only request, with its acceptance among our populace to be tested in the referendum.

I am pleading with you to take up our case by putting pressure on the Nigerian government to let Biafrans have the opportunity to decide whether or not to remain in this country where they are currently feeling not welcome, but are been killed by government and radical religious forces. The Nigerian nation is signatory to the UN pacts supporting the right a people have to self determination. Why are they condemning us and calling us criminals for asking for same? We shall be glad to receive help from your government in resolving this strident issue.

Furthermore, I want to plead with you to not stop the good work you are doing for all Americans and the world at large. Do not allow globalization which is geared at the re-colonization of the developing countries indirectly by world super powers to succeed. Countries are better left to make decisions favourable to the well being of their own people. The American government should keep withdrawing from any deal that tries to make America a money vomiting creature; it does not make the US less of a global leader, which is somehow acceptable to us. Some of these huge contributions your country makes are not really being used to solve the problems they claim to be using them to do. Instead, they are disappearing into the private pockets of bureaucrats in these developing countries. Instead, what we want in the developing countries, especially in Africa, is a constant call for fairness and freedom of self expression and self determination which are basic rights enshrined in international laws.

In relation to internal American affairs, I think you need to be more conscious of your safety as well. I know you are well protected, but America cannot afford to lose you to the bullets of ready assassins waiting to strike. We know they will not succeed, but the need to be careful follows the fact that most organizations in your country are under the control of Washington bureaucrats, many of which are not happy with your anti-deep state policies. Liberals have a way of imposing their choices on others and they can go through violence to achieve that. Be careful, for the sake of America's future.

Finally, Biafrans will be highly indebted to America if they help us to actualize our dream of a more peaceful and safe Biafran land. All we ask is to be supported in our call for a regional referendum and that the Nigerian government is pressured to abide by this international law concerning self determination. We look forward to working with the committee of nations in the coming years, even as we rise to our expected greatness where we shall stand side by side with the super powers in the world.

Congratulations once more for a victory well deserved.

Thank you.

Yours Respectfully,

Arinze Pius Has (ONWE)

ARTICLE TWO

The Hypocrisy of the American "Democracy"

Countries in Africa have over the years been struggling to institute a democratic process void of political manipulations and irregularities. Even their most widely accepted election outcomes still had pockets of irregularities recorded during the electoral process. Many times, the losing side of an election finds it difficult to accept the announced results. Some take to the streets in protests, and others go as far as taking their grievances to the highest judicial court in their country. At some other times, defeated incumbents refuse to leave power for the newly elected leader. Many times, there have been violent and brutal killings following such disputes.

The last election conducted in Nigeria in 2015 was widely applauded by the international community. This is not because there were no recorded irregularities in some places (actually, there were lots of malpractices witnessed in many places, especially in the northern part of the country were underage voters were registered and allowed vote). This applause came due to the fact that for the first time in the history of the country's fledgling democracy, since 1999, an incumbent president was supposedly defeated in the polls, and he bowed out without crying foul, despite the huge malpractices he knew occurred in the electoral process against his re-election bid. Today, Nigerians honour him for putting peace and safety of his people above his political ambition – no political ambition of any person is worth the blood of the citizenry at risk should there be violent eruptions as had always occurred in the past, something his political opponents seem to undermine.

As opposed to what is perceived of Africans when it comes to the conduct of democratic elections, America is known to have one of the best democratic processes in the world. The American constitution in itself is a power tool for true democracy. It takes the possibility of the big city elites imposing their candidates on the entire populace away and allows for a more widely distributed voting balance at the federal level through the glorious Electoral College. That's what true democracy means, but it does not end there.

Democracy cannot be said to be complete if the losing party refuses, directly or indirectly, to accept the outcome of elections that were conducted. The former president of Nigeria is celebrated today for choosing to step aside and concede defeat to his opponent without crying foul. He even went ahead to tell his party not to move in any way that will question the outcome of the election irrespective of what they believe may have been wrong with the polls. Today, there is no question or disputes as to whether the presidentlal election in the country was won or lost fairly. No protests or underground activities being sponsored by the defeated party or its candidate to question the legitimacy of the sitting president, at least, none that is known in public. And the country is a little more cohesive for that, I must agree, not minding the incompetence of those currently in power. Surprisingly and sadly for America, the world's leading democratic nation, the case is quite different since their last presidential election.

The big question is: why is the world's most amazing democracy struggling to completely accept the outcome of its election that was conducted according to the provisions of their most respected constitution months after the election was conducted? Why are they so vehemently questioning the emergence of the man now occupying their great oval office? Why are they acting like he seized power and not voted in by the people? Why are they using the mainstream media to undermine the legitimacy of their new president? Why has the part of the population that lost at the polls refused to accept their loss in good fate? What is with all the blames and counter blames on why it is the winner's fault that the loser lost? Where is the respect for the part of the electorate that voted the incumbent into power? Why is their right to choose their president being questioned? Where is the value and esteem of their constitutional process, if the defeated conceded defeat and turn back afterwards to cry foul play?

Do the American elites that lost at the polls truly believe in American democracy? By these I mean the old members of the long established political system; do they really believe in the government of the people, choosing by the people and for the good of the people? What are they supposing happened in their election that casts shadow on the legitimacy of the emergence of their current president?

Why are the sponsored protests still in American streets, with protesters sometimes turning to violence and directly or indirectly threatening the life of people with opposing views? Why do a couple of folks keep shouting down the majority present in town halls across US? And why do the mainstream media promote dissident views while at the same time ignoring the pro-government ones? These political games are too obvious to be denied. They are no signs of a good example expected of a major democracy that America claims to represent.

Though one might be right to call the 2016 presidential election in US a highly controversial one in terms of how the campaign period was so heated with both sides strongly attacking the other side with allegations of one form of past misdeed or the other, does this call for the eventual outcome of the election to be questioned? Why are they making the outcome of the election seem so much more controversial than the campaign, like their constitution has been so greatly mutilated by it? What are they fighting to establish: that the American president was foisted on them by a foreign government against the people's wish? Were those who voted him into power forced to do so? Where they bribed or cajoled by the outside government into casting their votes for the man in power? All these questions need answers as Americans today face the most serious threat to their democracy coming from within their political system. If answers are not provided to these questions by these Washington bureaucrats today crying foul, it will all boil down to the conclusion here that the much glorified American democracy is only a fiery tale. It behooves me to then draw the conclusion that the promotion of democracy around the world by the American government is nothing much more than a perfect imperialistic propaganda that keeps seeking to re-enthrone the long forgotten precedents of colonialism of the past against weaker countries of the world. It is a huge hypocrisy. And the countries of the world must revolt against such nuisance if ever attempted in coming years.

If America truly believes in their democracy, the

opposition party that lost the election handsomely, and are still losing since then in subsequent congressional elections (the four elections and one run-off conducted since Trump took office) should pull together with the party at the top, and without rancour accept the right of the electorate to choose their own president through the constitutional electoral process America possesses. They have to show respect to both their constitution and the people's right. It does not mean they must swallow hook line and sinker the policies of the current administration. It does mean they should quit the constant rhetoric that provocatively undermines and clearly questions the legitimacy of their constitutionally elected president. If these losers believe in America's democracy, they will not be out claiming that the man now in power is not fit to rule, and hence should be removed, when in essence he was duly elected constitutionally by the anti-establishment populace that thought him fit to rule. Things like these are only seen in third world countries where democracy is truly not what is obtainable even if taunted to be so practiced. Otherwise, what America claims to have is not democracy but hypocrisy.

A couple of other western and far eastern countries had conducted elections since the American election, and virtually none of the members of the big league to which America belongs who had an election are heating up today like America. France is a good example. No one is casting shadows at the legitimacy of the young president that emerged. Instead, France is moving on, despite the obvious division seen during the campaign trail, having settled down to allow the current government do what is best for their country. There is no hyped or cable news screen promoted disparaging of the president's fitness or credibility, notwithstanding the fact that much of what he had done since he took office opposes the beliefs of the side that lost. He still seems very much to be doing the same things the establishment that was pushed out would be doing had they won. No one is crying foul, even with reported foreign interference in the election process.

America has not been able to follow the example of the French people. They have failed to show us, by example, their total confidence in their democratic process, the possibility of someone with no previous political connections emerging to sweep powers off the feet of those who have been in the system for years. They seem to question the possibility of someone who during the campaign trail promised to make big changes to the norm winning fairly. It seems to many today that American democracy does not allow opposing ideas and policies to thrive. Otherwise, the man who won by promising to change the status quo, voted in by a populace that seem fed up by the existing situation, will not today be under fire for doing the things for which he was elected.

Some point at his moral values, but I understand that legality and morality are not the same. Morality is an individual's choice whereas legality is something everyone is mandated to abide by, as stipulated by the laid down laws of the land. Even America's constitution acknowledges this. So the accusation of the president being morally unfit is unfounded and anti-American. Virtually, no one would be morally fit to be in politics going by such precedence.

The right of a group of the populace, no matter how poor or uneducated, to have a say in the election of who controls the reins of power, seem to be thrown to the winds. They have been called a basket of 'deplorables', bunch of racists and white supremacists, anti-women and sexists, with all sorts of other unfounded titles for choosing to pitch their tent with the camp that ended up winning. These are not what a true democracy promotes. If the people cannot choose who they want in power without being questioned, then it is either democracy is nonexistent or it is a mere lip service description of a democracy look alike. Allowing minority voices without any form of intimidation, to participate fairly is what makes up a true democracy, especially if such democratic process turns out in their favour. These are what the American elitist group and bureaucrats are refusing to accept. If this is allowed to continue, then American principles will soon be history in the league of truly democratic nations.

If the American elite reject the emergence of an outsider to power in a democratic setting they had said was so right and should not be questioned when they thought they were going to win, it is the height of hypocrisy Americans may not know exists in their democratic system. These being the case go to only proof one thing that American elites do not believe in their democratic process unless it goes their way. This is more reason why the people should keep revolting by voting them out using the same democratic process they seem to have no confidence in once it does not favour them.

In essence, the populace, especially those not part of the big cities, should not be surprised to know that their country have been under the control of the few bureaucratic members of the established political system who see power as their birthright, just the same way it is obtainable in African countries. The only difference being the unconstitutional dictatorial tendency in the continent. Thus, African leaders are not standing alone in this huge political power play that questions true democracy around the world.

Americans should wake up and vehemently salvage the country from the hands of the politically correct, but self-centred and self serving political echelons of their country. This deep state is obviously in existence, and the future of America as a nation lies in the hands of the people to refuse to be cowed into accepting unfavourable political norms in the guise of leading the free world as peddled by these members of the shadow government. Voting an outsider who has the passion to return America to true greatness is a step in the right direction. It should also serve as an eye opener in deciding votes in subsequent general elections.

The excuse being given by the elite to de-legitimize a government put in place by the population should be completely treated with disregard. If anything, they should be booted out for such an un-American tendency that has become even clearer following the last presidential election.

ARTICLE THREE

How Fake is American Media outlets?

They are relatively fake, when compared to what true journalism stands for.

It is very evident that the liberal controlled US media is a charade. That would not be a conclusion too hasty, going by the incessant anti-Trump rhetoric that has been going on for over a year now. It has even grown worse since the man took office.

I have a simple question for those who may be fast to refute my conclusion: why does these media outlets portray the previous Obama administration as perfect, while claiming that the current one has nothing positive to offer the American people? To the best of my knowledge, it is not the duty of the media to determine how perfect or imperfect a government can be. They function only to ask questions and ensure that the public only receive true and unbiased reporting of government affairs. They are supposed to be a medium of interaction between the people and their government. They are not expected to take political sides, but simply side with the truth irrespective of the side that the truth favours. This is not what I have seen the American media do since Trump came into the political scene. The opposites are really the case.

Though not surprised, I heard someone on screen say recently about Trump being made to realize what happens when one chooses to fight an established system, directly referring to the mainstream media and the US spy agency, FBI. It is clear that this is exactly what the media in America is bent on doing in matters concerning Trump. They are determined to teach him that there is a section of the American society that is sacred and untouchable, irrespective of whom the populace put in Washington's oval office. If this is the new tenet of true journalism, I am yet to become aware of such.

In another instance, one of their own had also said that it is the duty of the media to decide for the people what and how to think regarding what is happening around them. This simply means that American mainstream media are constantly trying to control the thinking of the masses through the presentation of false narratives instead of real clear reporting of political and other related issues. With these instances, I would say that what is constantly on display on the screens of most of the widely watched American cable news outlets is an aspect of journalism that is far estranged from what true journalism should be standing for.

True journalism is not used as a form of making political statements, nor can it be used in driving political propaganda. Any form of political leaning is out of order with what the pioneers of modern journalism may have stood for. The bane of any media outlet is to take sides with any political party, be it the government in power or not. And the undoing is to refuse to ask relevant questions of these political parties and their government body if they are doing things that are not favourable to the population.

If the media's role in the society goes outside presenting unbiased accounts of government activities, reiterating the need to be more open for the good of the people, asking questions on issues that are not clear to the public assimilation and standing with the oppressed in speaking up against every perpetrators in government and private levels, then it is no longer fair but has begun to abuse the rights enshrined in media practice. The number one principle should be to present facts and figures as they are and let the people decide for themselves how to react to the facts, and then, equally present this reactions back to the government the way it is being expressed by the different groups that may have differing reactions to the same issues. It is not the job of a journalist to twist the facts the way it will favour any political party or group. It is not their duty to make any story look more factual or less concrete than it actually is. The media has no moral or legal obligation to lay unnecessary emphasis on political opinions, but let opinions simply be aired as they are. All these are simply the function of political advocates, not the media.

In the American media, I see two sides to every story: they are either favourable to the left or the right. It is only among very few that one sees fairness in media reporting in US. Most others want facts twisted to suit the side of the political divide they are clamouring for. Thus, one begins to wonder if media independence is truly something in existent. It appears they have been hijacked by the political side to which their bureaucratic and business owners belong. Sadly, the political undertones are just too alarming. More and more Americans are losing confidence in the media. Today, we all see media to only serve for entertainment, after which we take every other thing to be propaganda.

This precedence could be used to tag the American media as being Fake media. Fake media here refers to media that is not constituted and operated as the regular media should. By this definition, one cannot fault anyone who says the media in America peddles fake news, going by the fact that news is supposed to be devoid of second or third party opinion; news are reported as they are.

Coming back to the question I asked earlier concerning the reason why one government is termed perfect and another without credibility, American media have gone so far astray that I doubt that they do realize how much bad they have rendered media reputation in the eyes of the people. At least, I have followed the American media reports and reactions to Trump and other related issues over the past ten months, before and after the US presidential election; I have equally followed them keenly all through the Trump transition period and through the presidential inauguration to the present day of the president's less than 200 days in office, I can say with confidence that the liberal controlled

American media have not been fair to the trump presidency, even before his election. There has hardly been any kind of positive portrayal of this current US administration in the mainstream media. Watching these news outlets seems much more disgusting than watching an awkwardly produced fiction movie. They seem to swallow and mute all the good score points of the Trump administration, and instead, constantly hype the slightly 'questionable' reports about the Whitehouse. If one does not really know what is happening, and if one happens to be on the opposite side of the political divide to the presidency, one would be tempted to think that the Trump administration is out to send American to a hellish doom. They facts are so clouded with very strong false narratives that appears to have powerful backings from the purported shadow government Americans constantly refer to, which even past presidents seem to have alluded to in comments ascribed to them in the past.

Instead of asking questions that will require accountability from the government, the media have opted to asking questions that are in themselves questionable; questions that are based on already established political conclusions. I consider these quite hypocritical and absurd.

When Trump seems to do what is undeniably good and applaud able, they either give it one or two passing mentions or find some political reasons to downplay its importance. In such case, they usually turn to their political analysts in sympathy to the left. I sure doubt the 'political analyst' status of their panelists. Media political analysts are meant to be bipartisan in their thinking, and without surprise, that it not the case with these US media. They seem much like political affiliates to me, and this is very saddening.

The mainstream media in America demonizes every Trump policies that contradict the policies of the left and the liberal political thinking. They do not seem to care that these policies were the reason the president was elected in the first place. The question now is, do the media stand for the people or the political leanings of their owners? Why should the president not be doing what the people put him in power to do? Is there any reliable reason why government should abrogate the promise made to the people, which in essence is the reason for electing them? These goes to explain the fear people have about politicians making promises and not keeping them. Here is one willing to keep his promises, the media whose job should have been to encourage that these promises be kept for the good of the people are busy finding fault with every move the government makes in keeping with these expectations.

These things are what politicians do, especially in the developing countries of the world. The media has just to present facts without twists. Instead, they are busy playing as the medium for political propagandizing. I repeat, this is seriously sad to accept, but it is actually what is happening.

Like every democratically elected office holder, the new face at the top of America's political landscape should be accorded free and fair media coverage, not the covfefe treatment he is receiving every day. If you wonder what covfefe means, to my understanding, it is unfair media coverage of someone in a political office which is geared towards discrediting their competence and legitimacy to the political office. Hence, when the frustrated man in the Whitehouse rebounds, and fires back at the media with shouts of fake news, same media should cease to whine about it. After all, the man is a politician, and politicians are known to call people names, whereas the media is not supposed to be doing so. Doing so does not make him less presidential or less credible than his predecessors. Every human being reacts that way when pushed to the wall, especially when this is done constantly for no justifiable reason other than political grievances.

Despite this uncultured media bias against him following the campaign trail, Trump still emerged a winner with an overwhelming victory. By the continuation thereof, he has kept his winning streaks. If the media continue to fight him with the tools at their disposal instead of serving as checkmates for his government, it can only keep backfiring in their faces. His popularity is being boosted on daily basis, and the media does not seem to realize this, neither do they seem to care about their dwindling credibility to the public.

It is partly because of these incessant biased treatments of the media against the Trump Whitehouse that I conclude that they are a huge charade, and an absolute deviation from what is expected in journalism. The talk about the American media being a free press is a complete fallacy. If what is currently obtainable in American media is what free press means, then free press is a national disaster. For heaven's sake, what is so free about a partisan media? It is controlled by the political ideology of their owners. They are far from being free press, except that they are free to choose to throw away all known principles of media reporting and journalism.

How could it be press freedom that allows a media outlet lobby for top classified information from the spy agency of their country, and subsequently connive with some unscrupulous spies to illegally obtain this information? That is both treason, and aiding and abating of treason! I will be confounded to know that America's constitution permits such nonsense. Definitely, the American government and the citizenry are in jeopardy if that is the case! I hope America should put a plug in this.

The same people that are chasing the Wikileaks founder around the world for violating the constitution are putting up with similar acts by their mainstream media, merely because it seems to serve their interest. What is the difference between leaking private and classified information on the pages of the American regular media newsprint and doing same on the site of Wikileaks? The only difference I see is that the later is even fairer and more concerned about the American people than the mainstream media that are shrouded in secrecy in matters favourable to them.

Watching some of this cable news networks spin their stories, many of which involves making elephants out of flies, one feels sad and full of disgust for them. Sometimes, there are no flies even, but they always build one. One cannot help but bemoan the rate at which they peddle lies in the name of sourced information and the readiness with which they twist facts to suit their narrative. Some African media establishments are better off in this sense, even if they lack the resource and sophistications their American counterparts have.

The media in their anti -Trump campaign, have not

equally been fair to his supporters. They will let those who align with their narrative have free and uninterrupted comments on their space and time, but those who share contradictory views are usually cut short and cut out. I ask again: is the media not supposed to be neutral and truthful? Someone might claim they are not to be neutral, but just truthful, which is impossible. It is like saying the media can still be truthful without being apolitical. Those who believe in a truthful media without neutrality are dwelling on the edge of a steep cliff of media hypocrisy that will one day collapse into the gorge. It is stupendously wrong to think so.

The media by being neutral are bound to be true without twisting of facts or casting of politically motivated aspersions. American media scores 'direly' low on this scale.

Apart from being neutral and true, the media is supposed to be apt and ready to reprimand itself of erroneous reports, by rendering public apologies for such mistakes. However, the American media seems to be so absorbed in the quest to destroy itself that it does not publicly withdraw reports that are proven as false. Instead, they cease presenting the particular report and remove it from their sites. No apologies. How can such media outlets be trusted by the people? Rather than remove the huge specks in their eyes, they are fast to suggest to us that updates in facts coming from the Trump Whitehouse are contradictions of the previously released ones. The people in America and around the world sure know who to believe between Trump and the mainstream media.

When Trump calls the media Fake news, we all know what he means. This is one thing the media have not understood: the people believe Trump more than the mainstream media. Nothing even their biased polls can change this. These polls did not work during the campaign trail, nor are they going to work now. It is obvious that only a couple of Trump supporters have the time to devote to participating in polls that are meaningless and politically biased and more faults finding than solution seeking.

The media should try to regain the full confidence of the people before they go into oblivion in this rapid technologically advancing twenty-first century, where everybody is already turning to social media instead of the mainstream media, for daily information consumption. The little confidence they enjoy come from quarters that are aligned to the political ideology they represent.

Equally, they American media in its current state cannot start tutoring African media outlets or those in other developing countries of the world, where there seems to be more decorum in journalistic reporting than in America.

The concluding question would then be this: if the American media is not a charade as I have opined herein, why are they so political? Besides, many of them claim to be borderless, yet do not include the happenings in Africa in their reporting as much as they cover other regions of the world. Anyway, I don't want to go into the details here, since this is a book on America – the United States of America. But the dwindling reputation of these media outlets in America is SELF-INFLICTED. And they may never recover if they continue to toe this path that can only lead to their eventual neglect by the populace.

ARTICLE FOUR

The American Russia Story

The liberal American is mad at Russia: really? I don't think so. Instead, they are mad at Trump. They are hurt that trump won so resoundingly that they want to exhume a long cold hatred Americans had against Russia and use it against Trump's foreign policy which seems to want a reset with Russians. Now this: it is absolutely in America's best interest to reset its relationship with Russia. However, the shadow government does not want that for some reasons. Americans may not really understand this, but I believe that is what is happening.

Previous administrations before Trump had all attempted this reset, but it did not work out. Eventually, they easily threw the desire to do so to the trash and usually end up adding to the cold war going on. But, Trump seems more determined than the rest. That is why the deep state controlled Washington is on his neck with the Russian meddling nonsense. Yes, it's a complete nonsense. It is nothing much more than that.

There are basically three reasons why the left are tirelessly out with their Russia meddling story:

1.   To fight the reset in the relationship between America and Russia. Americans must know that this relationship is very important if America must reach its highest goal for greatness and achieve greater results in its fight against hostilities in the world. Though there is a group in America that thinks otherwise and would do anything, I mean anything, to prevent this from happening. Why they would be doing this, I don't really know.

2.   To undermine the victory of Donald Trump in the polls. They thought he was going to lose. When he won, against their predictions, they want to undermine that victory and attribute it to a third party influence. That is to say, they do not want Americans to see trump as the passionate hardworking American that means well for America and was able to win the heart of the common American who had been neglected for a long time by the city dwelling elites. You see, this

is actually a futility, since Americans love trump in spite of all those stupid false narratives. Don't you think so?

3.   Now, this is the most disastrous reason. They want to shroud more and more the secrecy surrounding the atrocities committed by the Clintons and their other accomplices in Washington. If what they are trying to hide here is ever made public (doing this will be very hard though), America will be in turmoil. As it stands now, they control the intelligence community. Until Trump has his own men in that community who are not loyal to the deep state, these truths will not come out. However, if the left continues to fight Trump with the Russia story, it will backfire in their faces.

There is only one way they can actually postpone the dooms day: by dropping the Russia hoax entirely and hope Trump is not angry enough at them to dig into this secrets. However, if they must keep fighting trump, then they should prepare to either rig him out (they can never win him) or kill him and equally kill the more determined Pence- a silent conservative with great passion for America's liberation from the influence of deep state elements. Now, killing both men would not be easy, and even if they pull it off, America will go to its second civil war.

In essence, the left are hurting themselves by fighting trump.

Back to our Russia story in detail.

Is Russia truly America's adversary? The answer could be Yes or No depending on who you ask. For me, the answer is: I don't really think they are. Yes, it is true they are competing with US on the world stage in many areas, but that does not make anyone an adversary. Competition is often encouraged as it boosts a party's ability to really be creative and productive. If anything, the competition posed by Russia, has driven America to push had at getting to where it is today in both technological and military development. So, I would consider it absurdity to refer to Russia as an adversary (in essence they mean enemy). They are using adversary to distract, but Russia is neither of those to Americans. Being friends will benefit both parties and the rest of the world more.

Another question: Does Russia really mean to oppose the leadership of the Whitehouse in the free world? My answer: who does not want to be the head of any group? Only a dummy does not wish for that. Russia are only hoping they can someday, overtake US. Now, I want to discuss as much as I can, the underlying truth in Russia-US relationship.

I may not have any solid material proof; I may not have any of the classified information; I may not be so sure about this, but I do not think Russia is any serious threat to America. Instead, I think America has been so distracted and misdirected by its very actual enemy. They are pursuing shadows instead of the real enemy,

I will begin with the supposed Russia meddling in US elections in 2016. Did that actually take place? Was Russian government actually behind the hacking of the DNC and co private servers during those election campaigns, in a bid to favour Trump? As it stands today, even with the so called evidence in the younger Trump's email as taunted by the biased media, we have seen no concrete or any substantial evidence to support that allegation. The left know this; the mainstream media too. If you ask America's intelligence agency, they will say, "Yes, absolutely". Then, ask them of the evidence that makes it absolute. What they supply are flimsy conclusions that can be debunked by even someone in grade three or lower. Hence, apart from the usually heavy worded accusations by people in the left and their sympathizers on the right, all we see is intelligent uncertainties- claim of Russian signatures being all over the place, which could have happened in any way that the Russian government may not be aware of.

The democrats and people on the left insists it's an established fact, yet they have nothing that can pass in a court of law, or anything that can be used to indict Russia in international court of justice. I bet you, if they do, it would have been leaked by now- because there are too many deep state controlled people in that IC than could stop that from happening. Today, American people are left hanging on a thin thread of uncertainties with no handy evidence to absolutely convince the average American of supposed foreign government interference in their country's election. Though, what we know was that the people who voted for Trump wanted him and could not be stopped by people on the left. Everyone is certain about this. It is clear that no one was approached by any foreign government to make them change their mind in favour of Donald Trump, then a candidate.

America's number one citizen who has access to

every (sadly not everything in the actual sense) classified secrets have actually not been convinced of Russian government exclusive meddling in that election. Remember, he has seen all the possible 'facts'. Being such an astute thinker, he was able to infer from what he know, that "nobody really knows" whether Russia really meddled. Americans should better believe their president. He has seen what no one else in the populace has seen, yet has his doubts about the allegations. Until they IC were able to feed him with the information that will absolutely indict Russia, Americans should stand with Trump in this believe,

As I noted earlier, if there is any solid proof of Russian involvement, America's leaky IC would have made all the favourable classified info public in their usual way. Until that happens, I choose to keep my bias on that topic intact. Luckily for us all, Russian government is vehemently denying these allegations. They are calling it a Russo-phobic tendency. Sometimes, they laugh at America.

Sadly, America seems incapacitated on this issue, very helplessly.

As if putting the blame on Russia is not enough, another obviously cooked up story came up. They are claiming, almost as if certain, that Trump's campaign had colluded with Russians in the alleged meddling. The sad thing is, there is as said before, no solid fact that Russians meddled exist, and they are still coming up with more allegations that are not provable.

It has been close to a year now since the Russia story started trickling in, yet nothing has been found to support it absolutely. Even with the control the deep state have on the IC operations, they still could not find anything. Rather, what we see is leaks on the private lives and communications of American citizens- scapegoats in the political "witch-hunt". Yes – political, that is what the whole story is all about, a political scheme. If it is not political, then, why is no one looking at the possibility of people in the left colluding with a foreign government to interfere in the last election to their own favour? Why is no one worried about the Ukraine contact the DNC had which is more provable, though they may have deleted all the possible links, judging by the denials coming from their quarters. They are good at cover ups anyway. Why is no one interested in checking the other sides of the Russian story, whether the Democrats have anything to do with that? It is possible this could all be a set up. In fact, it is more likely a set up than it is true.

Does the American constitution prohibit contact between its citizens and Russians – whether in doing business with her government or with private companies in Russia? Is it an abrogation of an American law for its government to decide to start a more cordial relationship with Russia? I do not know. I will leave that for you to answer as a patriotic American.

Moreover, the liberal owned mainstream media seems to be running the story even more madly than the aggrieved Democrats. They are all the same anyway. The media have been called the opposition party, and I think they really are. They are hyping the story; they have drawn harsh and hasty conclusions coupled with leaks and whistle blowing by treasonous folks. Yet, the story remains unchanged and liberals remain unhinged. I have only seen constant heating and cooling of the polity with the American Russia story. In all this, the American citizen is left confused – either in some uncertain doubt or believe.

Is the Russian story not made up as been suggested by some of us, including Trump? Without doubt, there is no substantial argument to negate this conclusion. Apart from political rebuttals from the opposition and media whining, and the usual rants of Trump is un-American and a Russian puppet, nothing counters the conclusion that it is all a made up story. So, emphatically, I would say this: this American Russia meddling story is a huge political witch hunt. It is a nonexistent story, unless it is proven otherwise. It came from a set of political losers who now feel robbed of their eternal right to dictate what happens in America.

Both the Russia story and Trump campaign's supposed collusion with them is an excuse to undermine the credibility of the American president – an outsider to the established political system in Washington. This is rather too ugly to acknowledge, but that is the truth in simple terms. If Americans fail to take this into consideration, they may continue to slide back into the throes of the deep state control of America's policy making. The gradual decline from real relevance in the world stage experienced under Obama as opposed to the smoke screen been taunted by the media, will continue. Americans should not be near a river and still allow themselves to be peppered. US is too advanced to continually be fooled by the elite, left or right. All the old political maggots eating up the American cherished values should be thrown into the trash of political nothingness. It's up to the people to decide.

Trump and his people should handle these issues carefully. People are already talking of perjury and obstruction of justice. It tells us that they know that the Russia story is a nothing burger, but are prepared to use it to make the Trump people to violate other laws of the land so as to put them out of favour with the people. Trump's people should be careful with what they say or do.

Coming back to the question of whether Russia is America's enemy, I will like to expand on it by expressing a series of personal reservations on the subject.

What does Russians want that Americans have? I doubt there is anything of much significance than what is basically the dream of every country in the world: countries of the world do want to be the leader of the free world, which happens to be where America is today. UK, Germany, France,

Japan, and particularly China, all want that position. Even Israel which is America's best ally. We all know that it is not a bad thing to want to be like or better than someone else. Why then are the Russians in America's perception different from other countries in the world? Russians are not even so close to Americans in economic values when compared with a country like China. Are they even in that big league of seven? China is closer to what Americans should be suspecting than Russia is. That brings us to the second aspect of these reservations.

From all indications, China, not Russia, wants that position America is occupying today. This is very obvious to everyone following what is happening in the world today. Who have not noticed China's attempt to step in where America is said to have supposedly stepped out of? Who have not heard of world economic summits organized by the Chinese government? To me, China is more of America's adversary than any country in the world can be. They are the next in economic prowess. In trade, they are the biggest competition. In fact, many American jobs have been lost because companies were moving to china because of cheap labour obtainable over there. In military, they are as much prepared as to warn America not to interfere in their affairs at the South China Sea. In influence, which African country does not have Chinese companies and government agencies swimming all over it? Even in technological advancements, they are gradually trying to outclass America, especially with their cheap technology. These things are so obvious, but so ignored.

China had in the last two years asked Nigeria to switch its official exchange rate from US dollar to Chinese Yen. Chinese language teaching schools are springing up everywhere in Africa. Surprisingly, no one in US seems to want to talk about this, at least, none that am aware of. I hope President Trump returns back to that campaign rhetoric of fighting China in their obvious economic war against US. See, China has the singular ability to cripple North Korea's nuclear threat to the world, which has constituted headache for America over the years, but they have not done anything serious about it. It means they are OK with it. If not, why are they so unwilling to do something about their trade/economic ties with NK. I would advice Trump, if am close to him, to stop expecting the Chinese to help you do anything. What the Chinese government wants is for America to fail at the world and local stages so that they can take their place.

The only thing I see with Russia in their relationship with the rest of the world is that they do not want to be controlled by any other country in the world. They want to stand as equals and not be seen as second to any other country. Like I said in my opening letter to the US president, I compared Russia to a small boy bully strong enough to resist being bullied by a senior or a bigger bully. This small boy is prepared to play any game that can make the bigger bully see him as someone not to control, but someone to treat as an equal even if it is obviously not exactly so. This is not what being a hostile nation or an adversary means. It is what every daring and bold nation in the world will do. For China, the case is different. China sees themselves as fellow big boys who want the same fame and bigger notoriety in the school.

For America to protect its place in the world today, she needs to stop fighting with the small boy bully Russia, and rather make them some kind of ally, being the big boy bully themselves. Russians would jump at that, because that is what they really want, to be seen as equals. Then, America must focus on China if it really wants to keep that position she is occupying in the world stage.

Russia has nothing to gain by fighting America. However, the bureaucrats controlling Washington and the billionaires with links to them, who have versed business interests in china do not want this to happen. Personally, I suppose they are the ones sponsoring the hyped Russo-phobic rhetoric on American soil, especially on the mainstream media.

Americans must wake up and arise if they want to take back their country. They must take the bull by the horn. They must keep revolting against the established system. They have to stand with Trump and with as many as are supporting his beautiful effort to restore America's glory. Even if US do not strike an alliance with Russia, they should not be calling names and throwing stones at each other. Rather, they should work together for the good of their people and the world. I believe this is the best way to be able to keep fighting the Islamic extremists that keeps rearing up their ugly head around the world. Also, Americans must band together in unity and cease from accusing one another. This is what your enemies want.

An America that is stronger internally is the America that will be stronger in the global setting. Anyone who has been weakening America's national affairs in the name of globalization does not mean well for America, and should be blocked out completely from policy making. It is in the hands of Americans, not Trump, to Make America Great Again. President Trump is only a signatory that will ensure that what Americans want is done. After all, that is the job he swore to do, which I believe he is ever ready to do, but only if Americans stand with him.

ARTICLE FIVE

Are Liberal Americans Crazy?

My answer: Not really all of them, but most seem to be, going by what is currently happening in America. I shall be referring to this majority whenever I mention liberals, or the left, except where it is stated otherwise.

No society functions without upholding a pact formed among a combination of diverse groups in co-habitation. This pact is formed through a harmonization of the various ideas emanating from individual groups in the society, and is geared towards ensuring the socio-economic development of that society. This development is maintained through the promulgation and enforcement of law and order. Acts and regulations are enacted to monitor the activities in the society among the differing groups, and they serve to ensure that no part of the community suffers in any form. Extremism in any group is dully checkmated to prevent such activities that are likely to tamper with the right of any individual group to co-habit with other groups. Fairness and equity prevents rancor and divisiveness among the groups. Where all these things are absent, the society is not likely to survive and thrive in the midst of the natural forces that often times turn out harsh and out of control.

For one group or faction in the society to insist on and impose its individual ideology on the rest of the society is inimical to the existence of such society. It even becomes more dangerous if this group also opposes other possibly better ideas from other groups from being considered, especially when these other groups are in the minority. Where this is not properly handled, the society is bound to degenerate into a situation of forced marginalization, rebellion, lawlessness and subsequently, chaos. A chaotic society is a doomed society, no matter the level of civilization it had attained. It is more likely to further slide down into a sorry state of complete anarchy. If nothing is done to quell the situation, the society is bound to eventually disintegrate into the individual groups in its makeup.

Sadly, no singular faction of any society is self sufficient enough to exist alone – ideas must be shared and resources must be pulled together among several groups. It is therefore the diversity of a society that ensures its survival, particularly in competing with its neighbours, and in fighting other environmental forces that may pose a threat to it.

Basically, there are two widely recognized groups that form a society – the liberals and the conservatives, usually referred to as the left and right. These groups serve their different purposes to keep the society coherent. The liberals have a likeness for new and untried ideas, and claims to believe in letting every part of the society co-exist with the rest with ease. The conservatives have a knack for ensuring that whatever is to be done does not violate everything that is deemed morally and humanly right. They seek to ensure that the society is not moving forward in the wrong direction or by doing the wrong things. A marriage of the two ensures the well being of the society. However, discarding the basic principles of any group results in division and clamour for change or resistance in the society. It is in this later condition that America, a nation of diverse cultures currently finds herself.

It is evident that in the past eight years, during the past US administration under Obama, American moral and human values were seemingly thrown overboard to give room for a more 'accommodating' environment. These saw the bringing into bearing and provision of constitutional support for views and ideas that were initially deemed immoral, ungodly and out of order with nature. These new provisions made lend more voice for a minority set of gays and other related sets in the American society. It gives them the right to openly associate and self-express among their kind. This new rights apparently allow people to differ to nature and openly practice what is deemed amoral without intimidation. The society had no problem with this, since it allows for more peaceful co-existence and gives people the freedom to express themselves.

However, the problem with these new changes was in their inability to accommodate the right of the other groups that have contradictory believe to express their own reservations openly. People should generally have the right to air and stand by their views so long as they do not trample on other people's right to express theirs. This was denied the part of the populace that do not believe in differing with nature or moral values. It then points out the anomaly of making one section of the society gain while the other section suffers to ensure the sustenance of such gains. This is a huge infringement on the right of these groups to equally differ. Hence, the liberal controlled government was not able to properly define the limit of legality and morality. This created a religious crisis in America.

Churches got sued for refusing to recognize what contradicts their traditional Christian beliefs. They were forced to do so or sentenced or fined for insisting otherwise. The same thing happened with hospital owners who do not believe in the differing to human nature as they were given no choice in legality to refuse to undertake such exercises. These thrived until the emergence of the current administration.

Largely, this article points out reasons that support the claim that the American liberal society is crazy in many ways. This have much been brought to the limelight following the election of Donald Trump as US president. The idiosyncrasies and the intolerant tendencies of the left have come vividly under the radar. Americans now know exactly what has been going on in their country for a long time now.

In every true democracy, the winner does not take

it all neither does the loser get annihilated. There is enough room for the inclusion of the opposition in policy making of the freshly elected administration. However, this cannot be possible if either of the sides is unwilling to work with the other. In America today, the later is the case, and the culprits are the liberals. When a liberal wins, the left are happy and peaceful. But their mood automatically changes when someone on the right wins. Unlike the conservatives who accept their fate and move to work towards winning in subsequent elections, the liberals seem to get unhinged and begin to look for faults to discredit the clear victory of the person they lost to. The winning of Trump, a complete political outsider took them by surprise, and seems to be the one that hits the liberal ego worse. The way they are heating up the American political setting these days serves to buttress this claim.

The liberals in America have sworn not to come to terms with a loss of an election they have officially conceded to initially. Several months have passed, but they seem to lack the courage to bury their hurt egos in the interest of the American people who had put the president into power. They have not ceased from heating up the polity. They have failed to understand that politicians who are unable to appeal to the needs of the populace get booted out of political offices. Coming up with one allegation or the other against the winner cannot help them. It can only make them continue falling out of favour with the voters. The false narratives they constantly create can best be seen as an attempt to undermine the right of the American people to choose their president. Indirectly, they are telling American voters who opted for President Trump that they were not in their right senses when voting for him.

All these name callings, throwing of tantrums, allegations of nonexistent violations of US laws, and shooting of opposition congress men are unnecessary. They are absurd and completely out of sync with what will drive a united society. Today, America is so divided, not because Trump won, but because his opponents in the mainstream media and the political establishment have defiantly refused to move on or truly accept the outcome of an election that was conducted constitutionally. It shows the height of intolerance that exists among the American left, the belief that if it is not their way, then it is no other way. The conservatives put up with an eight years long Obama violation of American cultures. Liberals should do the same here. If they don't cease from their resistance, instead of normal healthy opposition, it might take more than eight years before they can take that seat back.

Coming to the question of the credibility of the last American electoral process that ushered in President Trump, it is sad to note that the liberals are showing a double standard. They are the same ones who called Trump unpatriotic American during the campaign for saying he won't accept the outcome of the election if he loses. Every single liberal – political, media, private individuals, so berated the then candidate Trump for even merely doubting the democracy America has so nicely cherished for years. They claimed that his inability to have confidence in the electoral process and in American democracy, the best in the world, means he is not even fit to run. How could you think of challenging the choice of the American people, some on the left have wondered, even when Trump had actually being speaking up against possible attempts to rig the election against him. Such attempts have provable facts emerging today to support it.

Then, from the highest ranking political office holder to the lowest liberal in American streets, Trump was categorized as being anti-American and anti-democracy. Even the media could not hesitate to call this Trump's undermining of American values in the face of the world. Today, when the table has become turned against the liberals, after their false expectations were defeated, they are the ones doing everything they had called Trump names for saying he would do. They are the ones berating the American democracy before the rest of the world. They have so cast shadow on the credibility of the so much worshiped democracy in the world that I am beginning to think America is hypocritical with the claim of having the best democracy in the world. An electoral process is not truly democratic if a losing party fails to completely accept the outcome of the election and work with the winners in ensuring that only what is good for the citizenry is done. Instead, the American liberals are calling for resistance and impeachment of the one who defeated them with such a wide margin. This situation is only comparable to what is obtainable in third world countries.

On the accusation of misogyny being leveled against Trump and his supporters, we all know how misdirected it is. The liberals are proving to be the misogynists in America. They are the ones encouraging the religion that devalues women in the society. They are the ones calling women on the other side names and saying they are unworthy to own pussies just because they chose to differ and stand with the right. They are the ones constantly attacking a woman in the government just because she happens to be the president's daughter. They compel business establishments to boycott her products for no just reason apart from making political statements against her father. They are the ones fighting and booing the woman who is in charge of the Education body in the country. They are the ones sponsoring libelous publications gainst the first lady of the US. They are the ones asking stylists not to design her dress. They are the ones always trying to cast the first woman in America in the dark light. Who then are the sexists and misogynists in America today? The same liberals are. This is really crazy.

The liberals in America are the ones asking for easier sentences against terrorists and killers. They are advocating for the cessation of harsh ways of extracting information from detained terrorists. They are the proponents of the black lives matter in the US. However, research has actually shown that more whites have been killed by blacks than blacks have been killed by the white. Constantly, police officers have been killed and no liberal have protested against this in American. Do they really value human lives? I doubt. Are they not the ones advocating for the right to kill unborn babies, and that government should use American tax payers money to sponsor the same. They are the ones calling for unity when conservative politicians are attacked, but shout on top of the roof if a liberal gets attacked by even a psycho in the streets as though the right endorsed such attack.

The liberal Americans are the ones shouting racism every now and then. They are the ones trying to call every opponent white supremacists., yet are the ones who actually championed racism in America's past. Today, they are still the racists: blacks who have refused to accept an opponent that does not support their African American brother, Obama, during his presidency, are the racists today, including those who claim to have fought against racism in the past. What will make the liberal blacks in America shut their eyes to the ineptitude of the previous administration in standing for known American values if not racism? In the African continent, we view Obama as a colossal failure in American history. We loved him when he was elected, but he turned out to be more 'African' than he should have upheld American values. Major Obama policies actually favoured blacks more. Isn't that racism? The liberals are the American racists.

They are equally the intolerant ones, something they want to accuse the right for. The liberal society is really crazy. They refuse to accept other people's view in their bid to push their own agenda. Today, the divided state of America is so because the liberals have refused to tolerate the emergence of an outsider in their political scene. They see him as an outsider and an unconventional president, and want to treat him as such.

When private citizen Trump called Obama a liar who should not have been president for false identity, the liberals were up in arms against him. Today, they are the ones alleging perjury and calling for his removal from office, with still no proof. Some are even asking their terrorist partners to start a jihad against America's president. Who knows who the sponsors of terrorist organizations are? Who knows?

When the FBI were looking into Clinton's scandalous emails and gross violation in the handling of classified information, the liberals defended her and their liberal government helped to stifle the investigations and it was subsequently shut down without further digging. The DNC has equally refused to grant the IC access to their computers following the allegation of misconducts, and the liberals are OK with this too. Recently, the liberals were still the ones who accused President Trump of leaking classified information when just by exercising his constitutional authority he can choose to declassify such information when it is necessary for America's good. The accusation itself was false, and the liberals were the ones who still leaked and are still leaking classified information in the name of investigative journalism.

A whole lot of liberals have Russian links and have had several Russian contacts in the past years. No one wants to talk about this. What they want to talk about instead is who among Trump's team have had Russian contacts and had held meetings during the campaign as if American laws forbade them from interacting with Russians. If they are not on a witch-hunt with this Russia election meddling story, then they must broaden the investigation to also look into any possible collusion on both sides of the political divide. Equally, financial dealings of past and present political leaders on both sides of the aisle must be examined. The Russia meddling investigation should not be targeting only one political side. Also, the special counsel looking into the case must not have any traceable political ties with either of the major political parties; its members must be independent and apolitical in their leanings.

These are just some of the things that the liberals in America do that makes them look crazy to the world of conservative political observers around the world. This craziness seems to be a terminally incurable disease. The only task facing the well meaning American populace is to try as much as possible to keep these elements away from the corridors of power. Those who are already there can be voted out and replaced with more sensible Americans that want to work for the good of the country. If things are not done to stop the deep state controlled left, the American society will continue to degenerate and be portrayed as a thing of mockery in the world.

However, there are still a few sane liberals existing in America today, and I cannot end this article without blessing them for choosing to stand with the winning side even if they had voted against it. That is what it means to stand for American values. The rebellious Resistance will continue to lose, unless they return to common sense and be tolerant like the right and the rest of the more accommodating moderate left. God bless the American society and rid it of the deep state influence.

ARTICLE SIX

The American Politics of Hate and Media False Narratives Campaign

The emergence of President Donald Trump of US has opened up the American political can of worms. We are today seeing how American politics have been totally ridden with hate and intolerance. What should have been healthy opposition that would normally have ensured government responsiveness to social issues have turned up to be political suppression and witch hunting. What was originally seen as victory for the once neglected American middle class citizens have been turned into a barrage of hateful and divisive politicking. America, today, is a nation at war with its democracy. A citizen has described it as a revolution, not like America has had in the past. But, it is a revolution being spearheaded by the established government forces against the American people and their choice of leadership.

Without doubt, there is currently an ongoing scheme by the left to cripple government activities and subsequently suggest such as been as a result of the government's incompetence in handling American national issues. Sadly, this hate filled political left seem to be in charge of the government's intelligence establishments and the mainstream media. It is even estimated that out of the top 20 news outlets in US, only 5% - two of them – lean to the right. I am quite sure that one of this two, though pro-Trump, is not as biased in their reporting against the left and anti-Trump movement as their counterparts in the left are towards Trump and pro-Trump coverage. The rate at which information is dripping from the obviously porous American intelligence community shows there is gross incompetence in the way information security is been handled. Media houses seem to have connived with unpatriotic elements in the system to be perpetrating the felonious act of leaking information that should otherwise be privy only to people with some degree of security clearances. All these are being done in an attempt to discredit the sitting president.

The narratives in the majority left controlled media have no room for positive assessment of the current administration, no matter what it does. Every incidence is being hyped and has so been misrepresented as if the American people are dummies. Words and reactions of political opponents – the president and his team of supporters and aides, have been grossly misinterpreted with clear political mischievousness. Even body languages have been wrongly read and mostly associated with negative meanings. It's an all out war of building false narratives, with a hugely untrue claim that the government is been clouded with this narratives and are therefore unable to carry out other activities for the good of the people.

Stories upon stories have turned up and died down in what the left chose to call a scandal hanging over the government of the people. Over 80% of these stories have either not yet been proven or have been proven to be blown up stories and false propaganda that is used to cause political distraction. At the face of the American people have been thrown these lies and distortions and that without apology. Even parts of the citizenry that align with liberal thoughts are suggesting the politicking is becoming excessive. Some even acknowledged that it is making them think of switching sides as against the purpose of such negative propaganda, which was to make the people see the government as incompetent and shady.

The root of all these is the hatred the left seems to have for the Washington outsider currently in power. It is not even just that the power holder is an outsider; he is perceived to have the goal of setting at naught almost everything the political left seemed to have stood for. This though, is an inaccurate portrayal of the situation. It is very clear that this administration is only bent on changing the government policies that are not favourable to the people. These policies have only favoured the Washington bureaucrats at the expense of the American working class. For this, the system is hurt and is fighting back.

Surprisingly, there is nothing that is being done today that was not promised during the campaign trail. It is then accurate to say that the government is doing exactly what it was elected to do. If American people have not wanted the way things are going now, they would not have voted this government into power. The antagonistic left knows this, which is why they are out to cast the administration in the negative light as much as possible, but it seems they are only making matters worse for themselves.

The hateful left may want to use polls to determine how the administration is perceived by the people. However, they know they cannot risk being fair with it, because the outcome of a fair and equitable assessment would blow their mind and expose their agenda. Hence, they have resorted to doing exactly what they have been doing right from the campaign period – the use of biased poll results that have always turned out to be a false portrayal of actual street reality. These polls are biased in that there is no balance in the samples collected.

Since there are two major parties in the US with the population distributed mainly along this two divide, samples used in polls must be evenly distributed among this parties, without also neglecting those who do not have any political leanings. A situation where a poll is drawn from a sample that is not evenly distributed across the major party lines means that such poll is biased and therefore, an inaccurate portrayal of actual perceptions. Such poll results drawn cannot be trusted, especially when they are only used to advance the false narratives in the media that seeks to make it seem like the people are no longer in favour with the government, which is a pure political manipulation instead of a factual analysis of event that it is supposed to be. This only happens where there is political hate instead of healthy opposition.

The political left has always celebrated anti-government comedies and memes. They sponsor and provide blown media coverage for anti-American anti-Trump protests. Yet, they try to condemn and disparage pro-Trump memes and comedies that are being rolled out in their thousands daily by the American people themselves. They attack pro-Trump peaceful solidarity protests and turn back to claim that these protests are violent and un-American. One cannot but wonder how these hate peddling politicians and their media cronies want to make the people believe that pro-Trump demonstrators would turn violent against the government they are defending. It's all part of the false narrative build up being witnessed at its peak in this period of American history.

There are known incidences and stories that proof that what is happening in US today is sheer politics of hate, not democracy. The American people know this.

The story on the Trump inauguration crowd as presented by the media at the onset is both unnecessary and inaccurate. First, I must state here that the crowd in attendance at the venue may not be compared to those recorded in Obama's first inauguration. Obama's was obviously fuller then due to the historical meaning attached to his emergence. No one argues this fact, but that was not the argument the media were making. They chose to report that the venue had less number of people than expected. They used this narrative to suggest that Trump's winning of the election was not the choice of the majority of American population. At least, that was the message I got from watching CNN reports on the event.

This false narrative prompted the then newly appointed press secretary to come out with a broader portrayal, which claimed that the Trump inauguration viewership superseded any other in American history. This report was accurate as first stated, but the media debunked the authenticity, still holding their argument that the Trump crowd wasn't as much as Obama's as if anyone questioned that. They claimed that Trump's new administration was lying, when it was obvious to me then that the liars were the media. Why would they choose to only show aerial pictures of parts of the venue that were not filled up when in essence there was a huge crowd on grounds to witness the occasion? It is all part of the false narratives campaign, actually the first instance, against the new administration. It was completely unnecessary, and only showed how desperate the liberal media are in trying to discredit the support the people have for the presidency.

Besides, a great number of people who had

wanted to attend the occasion where kept out due to security questions following the protests and the time frame available. I also know that a greater part of the population that are pro-Trump stayed back home to watch the media coverage, some doing so due to fear induced by the media much blown coverage of the anti-Trump protests that were expected.

Coming to the issue of protests since the Trump emergence, it is so obvious that these have also been misrepresented. It might be true that there has been more anti-Trump protests that even had more participation than most pro-Trump demonstrations, but the media had failed to point out that these protests are usually sponsored by and have politicians taking part in them, as against pro-Trump marches, much of which were squarely organized by a team of Supporters of the Trump administration. This, actually, is not where I want to dwell on concerning this point.

I want to point out the fact that media clearly refused to give much cover to pro-trump rallies, except where these rallies collided with anti-Trump ones. The media hyped the anti-Trump protests in order to make it seem like a teeming population of the US are not in support of the president. They emphasized this narrative by not giving equal attention and reporting to pro-Trump rallies, many of which had drawn huge participation from around the country. This is part of the false narrative campaign the left is using their media organizations to push.

There was also the story of Trump breaking his campaign promise of draining the swamp when he appointed what the media called the Wall Street billionaires. These also was a false narratives geared towards challenging the presidents credibility in keeping to his promises. I will also point out here that the media has formed the habit of setting a double standard in the way they report Trump's execution of his agenda. When the administration seem to score a good point in making good their campaign promises, the media cries wolf that they are not trying to carry along the people who did not vote for him. On the few cases were Trump decided to reconsider his initial pre-election position on certain government policies after seeing the real conditions as they exist, the media would claim that Trump is backing down on keeping with the promise he made during the campaigns. It would be reported that he does not seem to have a clear agenda for his administration. This is absolute nonsense and lacks fairness on the part of the media. And, it is still part of the false narratives campaign.

There was also the question of timing in the firing of the former FBI director. Constitutionally, the president of the United States of America has the right to fire such appointed official at any time he so chooses and for any reason he deemed fit. He cannot be questioned for doing so unless there is any violation of the constitution preceding such action. Why the media made it seem like the president did the wrong thing – not even portraying it as the right thing, at the wrong time is very clear. It is still part of the campaign to undermine his presidency. They chose to conclude that the president did so in order to prevent the ongoing investigations into the Russian meddling hoax. Constitutionally looking at it, this claim is absurd. They forgot to mention that the president also had the right to decide who and what investigates what. After the interview when the president said clearly what he taught about at the time before deciding to go ahead with the firing, the left jumped at it and decided to misrepresent what he actually said.

In essence, what the president said in that interview was that he still had to fire Comey irrespective of the fact that Comey was heading the FBI that was looking into the Russian story. This, according to him was because he deemed that Comey was no longer competent to handle the FBI leadership. The media falsely reported that he said that his main reason for firing Comey was because of the Russian investigation that he wanted to forestall. Subsequently, the left argued that the Whitehouse gave conflicting accounts as to the reason for the firing. This was not what happened. The reasons presented were all as accurate as they were initially presented. That the president provided more information on the reason cannot be said to cancel the official reasons giving.

These narratives of the Whitehouse changing their stories frequently are false and inaccurate. What I keep seeing is updates provided upon further questions that are being asked. The media are the ones who keep trying to have the story get twisted to their favour. When they gather more stories, they claim that the Whitehouse story on the events is changing. The media has used these narratives to try and make the American people see the Trump Whitehouse as people not to be trusted, when in reality they are the ones that are losing the trust of the masses. The American liberal media lacks the credibility to cover political events accurately. You can see more of my thoughts on them in the third article in this publication.

When the president was accused of divulging classified information to the Russians, I personally saw it as a media effort to usurp the authority of the president by questioning his right to exercise his constitutional obligations. Though, the American people may have taken it as one of these media hysteria, but it was truly a quest to undermine the legitimacy of the president.

It was those who accused the president of violating a nonexistent law that actually violated the American constitution by revealing classified information to the public, thereby putting the American community and their allies at risk. Apparently, the story was not carried for long by these media outlets like they do with others because they realized their huge misconduct. However, no one has apologized or seemed to be perturbed by that incidence. It was a show of madness and journalistic recklessness in reporting security sensitive information. The Trump Whitehouse should seriously put into place a measure that can help plug these careless leaks of information from the intelligence community in US, particularly the FBI and CIA- two of the American spy agencies hugely controlled by the deep state. These organizations are becoming more political than the liberals are hypocritically claiming they should not be in other not to favour the Trump administration.

As a matter of fact, the hate politicking in US today is mind boggling. The system has a total display of its displeasure with the Trump administration on American screens without control. Is it the refusal to confirm the nominees in a bid to keep Obama hangovers in charge of some government affairs? Or the lack of contributions to setting right the failing healthcare system that Americans voted Trump for? Or even the blockades of the administration's efforts to checkmate the possible import of terror groups into the US through regular immigration and refugee programs? These fights are not for the good of the people. These fights are being waged by self-serving bureaucrats who do not care about what the people wants. This is not the opposition expected of a healthy democratic state like US. It demeans the image of the US in the eye of the on looking world. It speaks of desperation and lack of fair play. It portrays a strong political intolerance and a usurpation of an authority that is supposed to be the people's.

Trump, like every other human on earth is not perfect. Sure, there are no perfect humans in existence. He has his individual pattern at play in the way he handles politics. I agree it is unconventional and out of sync with the established system, but are the people complaining? No. At least, those who do could not keep him out of the Whitehouse. He is aggressive and 'excessively' eloquent. He possesses the ability to sway the people to his pattern of thinking without bordering about at whose expense he is doing so. He is so self conscious and hard at fighting that he kicks back at every attempt to question his integrity. America had never seen a man of his sort running for that high position before. Surprisingly, he appealed to them more than what the system had to offer. Trump has not changed much from what he was before the people chose him at the polls, and he has no promise of changing. The people who voted him do not seem to care much about this. What they care about is the fact that he is working hard as ever to fulfill everything he had promised during the campaign. Annoyingly, the political establishments in Washington are not giving him the support he needs to carry out the agenda for which he was sent to the Whitehouse. To me, this is not a problem for Trump. It is a big problem for those resisting him which they may not realize now, but will be shocked to discover at the coming polls.

The system had refused to pay attention to the wave of support for the president on social media during the campaign, even though common people like me saw it and knew then that Trump was unstoppable. Today, that wind is growing fierce and all the media still have to say is a repeat of the campaign miscalculation: ignore your multiplying social media following and look at the biased polls from anti-Trump media houses? I see this as a battle between the people and the system, with Trump on the people's side. It will be a huge blow on the system when the time comes.

This politics of hate, or loving Trump's hate, is like dancing on shifting sands. Americans are geared up to take back their country, and are prepared to help the establishment sink deep in that sand. Those who instead of bringing fair opposition and contributions to the programs of the Whitehouse are threatening to impeach and fight till they see Trump removed are obviously not going to see the end of Trump's tenures still sitting in their current political positions. The Trump movement is unstoppable. As far as from Africa here, I can see it. I can feel it. I can sense it; I can read it and I can imaging the huge blow it will inflict on the system. American politicians should learn from what happened in France and sheath their swords and come to the table for the good of the country. Except they want to use the bullet to achieve their goal, which will lead to greater chaos, they are bound on a futile mission. If Trump survived even when the system was in power, what makes the political establishment think he will fall when he is in power?

I believe that Americans know where to stand. It is either the people and their president or the political echelons and their Wall Street bureaucrats that will hold the right to control activities in Washington and on the Hills. I rest my case on this issue here.

ARTICLE SEVEN

Terrorism and the Question of Refugees.

Terrorism has plagued the world for years now, particularly through radical Islamist extremism. One question that has not been answered over the years is where the root of this Islamic radicalism lies. Though one can argue that Islam is, by itself and like every other religion widely acceptable in the world, a religion of peace, but that does not leave some doubt in the minds of a lot of people in the world. Its leaders claim to openly preach peace and religious tolerance. However, these does not answer the question of why much of the world's terror incidences are carried out by radical Islamic groups; why they are radical about Islam to begin with; and why they also strongly believe to be doing god's will as enshrined in their revered canon, the Quran. More so, when many of the perpetrators on the field usually turn out to be people who interact with others in day to day activities, and live and worship among the population. To isolate these individuals from the communities where they dwell, among the regular people, before carrying out their terror acts seems to be a hugely impossible task for the leaders and security forces in those places. One can only begin to wonder the part that Muslim community leaders play in the curbing of terrorism emanating from their neighbourhood. I will discuss these further later in this piece.

Another question posed would be: what does the holy book of Islam say about what its adherents do? Does it condemn or encourage those dastardly acts of inhumane human induced disasters? I leave the answer to these questions for the experts in Islamic studies.

As pointed out earlier, over the years, terrorists have always claimed to be doing god's will by carrying out the various horrific bombings and killing of innocent Muslims, Christians and political establishments that we have continued to witness all over the world till today. They claim to have the divine mandate to annihilate the infidels, referring to individuals of other religions and more moderate Muslims in the world. They claim that civilization, particularly western ones, is anti-god and therefore unacceptable or should be discarded completely by Muslims and the world which must be fully Islamized. This movement have constantly been termed an ideology other than what the perpetrators prefer, which seems to be more like a religious war with scriptural approval to infiltrate and conquer every part of the world and make everyone abide strictly by some laid down religious rules that some adherents believe are too harsh to be part of their call.

I will have to formally begin by providing my own definition of this monster called terrorism. It is the inhuman act of causing death or harm to helpless individuals or entities in a very violent way with a guise to make political or religious statements. The methods used vary depending on the resources available to the perpetrator(s) involved and the nature of support they have from some other favourable body plus their particular intention and choice of target. The tools are usually ranging from the use of pocket friendly knives to sophisticated equipment such as a set of bombs and ammunition. These tools can often be purchased from the regular stores in the neighbourhood or from illegal dealers or even from dubious government officials who have legal access to them. Some can even be handmade following a series of tutorials that can easily be accessed online today.

Different terror groups or individuals might have different motivations, which can either be religious or political. The most frequently witnessed motivation is religious, though this is also shrouded with political undertones that may not be in the public glimpse. Notwithstanding, the actual individuals who are used to carry out these terror activities are basically driven by radical religious ideologies than any other motivations being suggested anywhere else. That's is why it is often not inappropriate to call terrorist groups or individuals radical Islamist extremists.

There are, without doubt, known and unknown government establishments that sponsor terror organizations for political reasons. These establishments either profit directly or indirectly from the mayhem in a political or economic terms. This is basically one major way terror activities get financed. Other ways include personal income earned by individual perpetrators, or donations supposedly gotten for good purposes but were rather meant for terror. I should also point out here that there can be established business ventures that are owned by these dark organizations, which they run using third parties to avert suspicions of any kind. In such cases, finances are moved in a very well coordinated manner that little or nothing is known about these involvements. All these exist to help terror thrive. Government bodies must wake up and properly monitor companies and organizations operating within its borders.

How can this menace of terror be curbed in our societies? There are many ways these can be done:

First, the refusal of the global community to associate terrorism, in clear terms, with the basic motivation which is radical Islamic ideologies related must be stopped. If much of the terror being meted against humanity, especially since the dawn of the twenty-first century, have been linked to Islamic extremists, then we should call a spade a spade. If people hang on religious teachings as an excuse to commit terror, such teachings should be looked into instead of being excused as being merely wrongly held religious ideologies. Are these people being fictitious as to their claim that their religion requires them to do these deadly stuffs that only make humanity to exist on the edge. I know the political watch dogs in our world will frown at this, but I must make it clear that this world will never be rid of Islamic linked acts of terror unless we all agree to take the bull by the horn.

Next, the best way to start effectively working towards fighting terrorism is to take a look at the grassroots; these terror perpetrators live in our communities. They walk in our streets, live in the same dwellings as we do, go to the same markets we go to, hang out in the same neighbourhoods and most times attend the same religious programs we attend. There are programs that can be put in place which will allow community and religious leaders to be capable of giving proper accounts of people who are under their daily, weekly observations. Taking it further, even kinsmen and family members can be made to understand and be able to account for the activities and everyday whereabouts of their members.

Generally, the community can be on the lookout for one another and be able to report to the authorities activities and ideologies that are going on or being expressed by some people in the community. If grassroots lookout is made to be very effective, it will make recruiting new members difficult for these terror groups. It will also help to detect individuals who may have personal motivations to indulge in acts of terror, hence curbing the risk which they pose, and equally help in rehabilitating them and offering them help where they need it.

Government efforts at the grassroots should also be directed towards ensuring that members of the local communities who are of the working age are gainfully employed. Equally, every existing group or association in these communities must be known and dully registered, and their activities closely monitored constantly, especially religious organizations. Religious leaders should be able to properly give account of the people who come to their places of worship. They should easily tell a new face from the old ones. They are to equally monitor the activities of their members and know as much as is possible, their day to day engagements.

In addition to being accountable for their members, religious leaders in every community should play the role of disabusing the mind of their people of any radical ideology that may be filtering into their minds from outside forces. Proper religious orientation and re-orientation should be carried out on a regular basis. Members should be made to understand the extent of what they believe in and how far it cannot go. No form of inciting rhetoric should emanate from these religious leaders.

Religious authorities should equally monitor the activities of those leaders they have assigned to overseer individual places of worship to ensure no negative influence comes from them to the worshipers under them. Bad elements should be removed and handed over to local authorities for further investigations and subsequent rehabilitation or prosecution. If there are perceived grievances, authorities should step in to proffer the right solution to these problems and prevent further escalation of tensions that may be in place already.

As information comes to the authorities from the communities, they should not be neglected or treated with recklessly. There have been cases of terror attacks by individuals in UK who were said to have been previously reported to the security agencies for their questionable activities. If the security forces have kept their radar actively open in monitoring the activities of these individuals, they would not have succeeded in carrying out their terror attacks. Hence, security forces in towns and cities should always be on a high alert, especially in those places where there have been common incidences of terror. These force men and women must be properly trained to handle terror prevention and control of difficult situations. They should equally be well equipped with the necessary gadgets required for both the gathering of information and cracking down on perceived hideouts of suspected terror groups in the communities where they are posted.

Intelligence gathering on terror should be of paramount importance for the local security forces. These should not be left for only a group of people in the force at the federal or state/ provincial levels who may not even be out there in these various communities to know what goes on there. Security at the grassroots is made easier when adequate security measures are taken at that level to work with the community leaders and other stakeholders. The force men should be able to interact with the people at this level, and probably know people and what they do from day to day. Government should not only be ready to send in forces to quell already occurring attacks, but these forces should be handy in those communities to prevent the attacks from even taking place. There is no way security forces will be handy at local communities and the rate of terrorist attacks in these communities will be going up as they are in some parts of the world.

In recruiting members of these security forces, government should be apt to carefully examine the individuals being recruited. We know there is the likeliness of security forces that protect communities being infiltrated by bad elements. It is the duty of the government to know the backgrounds of people they are employing and training to the last information. People should not be admitted into the force without the authorities consulting with the community leaders where these individuals lived. There have been incidences where security personnel had colluded with terror groups to carry out their attacks. There are even cases where a security officer had been the singular perpetrator of such terror. All these can be prevented if the appropriate measures are put into place for the recruitment of force members.

One effective way to curb the spread of terror activities and their perpetrators to countries that would otherwise not be easily affected by it is to put into effect a serious vetting process that clearly examines the people who seek to move into such countries. The green light will be specifically beamed on those individuals who are nationalists of the most terrorist prone societies. It, however, does not have to matter the country through which they are entering. Terror organizations are known to disguise their members as ordinary individuals with simple reasons for moving into a new country. Asking questions of everyone does not have to be seen as a nuisance. Subsequently detaining those with questionable backgrounds should equally not be seen as discriminatory. All these excuses seem to me to be the kind of things that could be heard from terrorists' sympathizers and sponsors.

The west today have suffered serious threats to its existence through the massive and obviously unchecked intake of immigrants from these terror prone countries. German police recently reported how terror organizations are smuggling in their members into the country through the refugee intake program of the government. Refugee intake is not the best way to solve the world's refugee crisis. In fact, it is the best way to encourage the intake of terrorists into countries that would otherwise be safe. It should be noted here that the main reason terror organizations are making the east unsafe is to bring about the spread of radical Islamism. They love the intake of refugees into western countries, and use the same medium to ship their members into those countries. This should not be argued. It is the reality.

There are other measures that can be taking to handle refugees. First, the creation of safe zones in these countries can be handy. Secondly, the need to embark in an all out war to defeat this terror groups so that people in these countries will have no need to want to leave their countries.

Also, completely banning the intake of refugees into other countries can even help in bringing the war to an end even faster. It will make the individual governments in these affected nations to dully wake up and salvage their country from the throes of terror perpetrators. It will equally make them put into place, measures to curb the spread of this activities in their communities. To me, this is the ultimate way to ensure that terrorist organizations are nailed.

US and other world powers like Russia must team up and assist local forces in the east just as they are currently doing. The use of local forces, not rebel groups, has proven to be very effective in the fight against terror in the east. Equally, these local forces can be assisted in maintaining order in societies where terror organizations have been expelled from to avoid a further collapse of those communities. These super powers can equally help these countries to develop orientation programs for their citizenry to help curb the spread of radical ideologies. This battle can be very easily fought on the internet which seems to be the basic method terrorists use in recruiting members from around the world, as against using the porous refugee programs to spread their members.

I think there should be a set of words that must be seriously censored from being used on the internet in specific ways. It is the responsibility of the government to put these measures into place. They should demand that internet and social media companies do exactly what they are required to do to help.

Countries should desist from arming non-government forces in the guise of fighting terrorists. These non-government forces so armed can turn around and use this weapons to fight the government, thereby creating another crisis that could allow terror groups to develop and function. They might even further turn around to use these weapons to advance their own interests which might not be for the good of the people of those countries. I strongly believe that arming non government forces is synonymous with arming terror groups. These militant organizations are self-serving and cannot be easily restricted or sanctioned in the case of any eventuality.

Apart from the regular combat against known terror organizations, the international community should collectively ban organizations that promote radical religious ideologies. These organizations may not be openly up in arms, but might be encouraging terrorism directly or indirectly through their activities and regular rhetoric. There should be no hesitation in designating these radical organizations as potential terror organizations, and equally have their activities closely monitored.

Severe economic sanctions should be implemented against states that are known to sponsor terror groups secretly. Those who do the sponsoring openly should equally be designated as terror states and subsequently treated as such. Any known companies that are known to be financing terror groups, directly or indirectly should be closed up. Owners of such companies must equally be detained for further questioning and probing.

Employing diplomacy in the handling of terror issues should be greatly discouraged. Diplomacy belongs to political governments and not terror groups. Government bodies should not negotiate with terror groups, except where human lives are in jeopardy. Any pacts reached must only be streamlined towards saving these lives, and nothing more. Otherwise, what terror groups require is the use of force.

I may not be a security expert, but I believe that if the measures suggested in this piece are put into place, it will help in solving much of the problems the world is facing today with terror attacks.

ARTICLE EIGHT

Americans MUST Decide the Way Forward

What exactly does the average American want from their government? What seems to be the reason why the American people are fed up with the system in place in Washington? What changes do these people of diverse cultures want to see brought to their country? Why did they choose to revolt by voting in an entirely new kind of politician into the Whitehouse during the last presidential polls? One cannot know the answer to these questions without paying attention to what the American people themselves are saying.

Having been following the average American's line of thought as expressed on social media and mainstream interviews and debates, I believe the average American wants his country back in pursuit of matters of national interest, not in the hands of bureaucratic globalists and their Washington lobbyists who want to milk America dry in pursuit of global business establishments. They want the interest of the country at the forefront of every diplomatic efforts or bilateral trade deals the government is embarking on. They don't want policies or agreements that enrich foreign organizations or goals of foreign governments at the expense of the well being of the employable American citizen. They don't want their wealth being thrown away in the name of charities to some parts of the world where this dollars end up disappearing into the private pockets of corrupt politicians in foreign nations, especially in Africa, my politically derelict continent.

Americans want a country where there is job for every person who has reached the working age, and where American companies stay in America, produce in America and hire Americans. They want a country where every industry is booming and the government is not using its power to make policies to hurt these industries. They don't want to see their jobs being taken by illegal migrants or been let to go to cheap inexpert labour overseas. They want companies that have left the country for various reasons back in their country to create jobs for American people. Americans want to see small businesses grow big and big ones stay alive untouched by the taxing system in place. They do not just want to be world's economic power; they want to remain so and have the economy benefiting the average American citizen.

Americans want better tax reforms that will allow these jobs to stay in America for Americans. They want the rich and poor of the American society to be treated with equity. They don't want to be working to run the government and at the same time be enriching the few billionaires of Wall Street who are controlling Washington. They don't want to use their hard earned money to carter for illegal immigrants and continue to take care of a teeming population of refugees many of which turn out to create problems for American communities. They don't want a country where they are forced to use the tax payer's money to sponsor people who want to kill innocent unborn babies. They want a workable tax reform favourable to the everyday American person, and they want what is fair on the American tax payer in the way their money is being spent by the government, especially on the global stage.

Americans want the government out of the control of their healthcare. They want to be able to choose their healthcare, and they want it to be affordable to everyone and not just to the rich or the politicians who do not even have to pay for it. They had a supposedly affordable healthcare imposed on them which turned out to be too expensive that the average American cannot even afford to pay for it. Instead, what they want is health insurance programs they can choose to have and which they can afford. They want healthcare that will be easily accessible to them when they need it, without having to queue and die while awaiting their turn for days. Every American today agrees that the existing healthcare system is not working; most want that system completely repealed and replaced with better people-centred healthcare program. Also desired is a better care for American veterans and their families.

More importantly, Americans want a more secure border, and a more vetted immigration process that does not permit terrorists into their country. They want their government to make sure that the people coming into their country are ready to abide by American laws and live by American standard. They don't want criminals coming in when they are trying to tackle the ones already in the country. They want a border wall powerful enough to keep out hoodlums and drug peddling gangs from neighbouring countries entering into US. They want illegal immigrants sent out, especially every one of such who have known criminal records. The safety of their lives and properties is paramount to the sustenance of the country's economic growth and should not be taken for granted.

Americans want justice in their judicial system. They do not want the government treating highly placed high level offenders differently from the average American. They want tolerance in their communities. People want to be able to stand for what they believe in without having to be afraid of being harassed by those with opposing views.

Among all, every patriotic American wants to see their country back on the track to greatness. They want their government to only work towards MAKING AMERICA GREAT ALWAYS. They do not want their government interfering in other countries' domestic affairs, whether it's by influencing their election to favour American political interest or toppling sitting heads of state by arming rebel groups who end up misusing this arms. Americans do not want their country beating the drums of war with any other major world power. All the want is to make America great again, and at peace with other nations of the world.

Without any iota of doubt, to the average American, Trump is the man fit for the job of making America what it is supposed to be. They see him as an outsider to the rot in America's political system. They see him as been more at home in relating with the everyday American. They see him as a champion of the people's course. They love him and they love his unprecedented way of doing things.

They view Trump as the wealthy American political outsider who is tired of the system and wants to help Americans bring about the change they so desire. Money was not his driving force, not even fame – he had a large dose of both as a private citizen. Instead, he has a very obvious passion for America's greatness, which suffered under the previous administration. He sought to bring back the glory of a country buried for eight years of moral and national starvation.

The American people were fed up with the established system long in place. They chose to stand with the new hero who wants to help effect a positive change in the system. They ignored the political war that was waged against him by the establishment and the mainstream media during the campaign trail. He was called a freak and a loser by the media, grand-stander and opportunist by the bureaucrats, and was said to be unfit to even be a presidential candidate let alone occupying the seat by the political power blocks of Washington. He was blackmailed by the media and the opposition. They sought to pit him against the women, the minority groups and the African-Americans in the country, but they failed to stop the people from standing by him and putting him in power to fight for their course. He stood alone, but only with the people.

In spite of all the tools at their disposal, the

establishment could not stop the people's choice. Against all negative poll results peddled in the campaign trail, the people's man won the presidency, chosen by the people, determined to change the face of the straying American politics and world view.

As expected, the establishment is aggrieved by not just the people's rejection of their candidates, but also their choice of the derided newbie. They have refused to sheath their swords and wait for another opportunity at the polls. They have resorted to the campaign of calumny and use of false narratives in a bid to run down the new government. They are working tirelessly to undermine the legitimacy and the credibility of the new administration. Surely, the American people are witnessing these efforts by these politicians and their media sycophants. They know that these people are the enemies of the American people. They see all their efforts at bringing down the president as an affront on the

American populace that put him in that office. Hence, it's an all out war, a battle for supremacy between the system and the people.

It is an onus task upon Americans to, therefore, completely rid themselves of these political monsters that want to run down their government. They should be prepared to take this battle to the polls. There, they are unstoppable once they rally around the president, in spite of all false narratives rampant on the mainstream media aimed at casting doubt on the president's credibility. The greatness in America's future now lay at the hands of the electorate.

Americans must also realize the threat against their president as posed by the establishment and their stooges. The increasing love-Trump's-hate promotion in the mainstream media and the hate filled social media rants of the opposition all point to one direction: remove the president from that office by any means, good or bad. This does not rule out assassination. It has been rumored that there are secret plots to assassinate the president, and it looks to me that the Americans are not scared of this. Anyway, they should not be scared; after all, the president of the US is the safest man on earth. However, Americans must remember that the people in control of their government agencies are not loyal to the president nor they constitution that brought him into office. They are loyal to the deep state that has been controlling Washington over the years. To this sinister group, Trump is a problem that needed to be gotten rid of and they are prepared to go to any length to do just that. One does not have to wonder how this can be pulled off, but we hope such would not see the light of day.

From the campaign period up until this day, verbal, animated and written threats have been promoted on liberal owned mainstream and social media. Support for Trump has obviously been stifled to some extent, and anti-Trump rhetoric has continued to have field day. The recent shooting of a GOP congressman is a proof that the left can go to any length to stop the people's president. I must say this here, there are liberal stooges determined to take the fame for assassinating the president of the US. They are prepared and willing, ready to take advantage of any loop hole in the president's security detail which may be created intentionally or by error. There is no amount of sophistication that can be 100% proof against desperate liberal assassins. Americans must keep their eyes and ears open, and shun social and mainstream media threats. American intelligence agencies must stop taking for granted verbal threats to the president's life. Animated or acted threats in the entertainment industry must be taken seriously and dully censored. Hateful movements should be closely monitored.

If anything does happen to the president of the people, am sure Americans will revolt. It will be the doom for the United States. The division in the American society today is a sign of a country on the edge of a precipice. The politicians, especially the left leaning ones, are choosing to bask in the euphoria of resistance instead of returning to the healthy opposition for which a democracy is known. They are only interested in pleasing campaign donors more than the people they are elected to serve. They forget that harming a man that a victorious majority of Americans see as a political messiah will only serve as a referendum on the peace and existence of the nation. If that happens, America may never recover. America is not immune to disintegration. No nation is.

I want to, therefore, plead with all Americans to put their differences aside and unite under the president. Politicians calling for resistance do not mean well for America, but are only out to meet the global needs of their American and other secret foreign bureaucratic sponsors. They are political power mongers who believe politics is reserved for them and their deep state members. They do not pursue the interest of the common everyday American that the president had stood for since he took office. These are the ones to be flushed out of America's political system. They have only always promised one thing while they do another when they come into office.

President Donald Trump has shown within the first few months of his presidency that working for the good of all Americans is why he had joined the race in the first place. He should be supported and allowed to implement his agenda that is focused on taking America back to where it belongs. Though the mainstream news media may not cease from building up their false narratives as evident on screens reaching beyond American soil, they are bound to keep failing while the American people and their president continue to win. So, stand with the call for a Greater Nation. A nation that is weak within will eventually lose control without; it is time to make America strong again on the inside by ensuring national interests come before global agenda.

Trump must be protected. He should also be assisted. The media should be thought what it means to keep playing the card dished by their masters. Americans must boycott those of them who have refused to practice true journalism. Neutrality in media coverage allows for true presentation of facts in news reporting. Covfefe incidences should cease. Neutrality means standing with the people and not siding with any political party for any reason. The power to choose the politicians in power belongs to the people; it is exclusively theirs under the constitutionally recognized democratic process. It is not for the media to support or oppose the government. Their mandate is to speak the diverse minds of the people and demand that the government do what is best for the country. The American media should learn to be free, fair and apolitical. This is what the Americans must ask for and insist on.

The future of the most powerful country in the world now lies in the hands of its people. Whether America is allowed to be swallowed up by hate and division, and by the global one world order or not is up to its populace. Whether the existing self-serving political system in place succeeds in their sinister agenda or not is up to the everyday American. Whether the media should continue to spurn the true choice and need of the people, and continue to gloat in their disparaging efforts against the constitutionally elected government of the people or not is solely the people's decision to make. Every true American must awaken to the reality of the times and put hands together with fellow patriots to salvage their nation from the throes of the evil that have become obvious in this day.

This is a battle to be fought at the polls. It is a battle to be decided by votes. It is a call to drain the swamp, which only the people, and not their government, can do. It is only when these battle is fought and won (the people never lose), that the cry to MAKE AMERICA GREAT AGAIN can succeed. Until then, the ball is in your court, you highly esteemed American patriot! Take the horse by the reins and stir it to victory. Only then can you sing the victory song in peace.

END NOTE

If America fails any day, it is not due to bad leadership, but due to the inability of its people to awaken to their constitutional responsibility of choosing better leaders. Better political leaders are those who put the interest of the electorate above their personal goals.

Trump has shown America the way they seemed to have lost in the recent past. If the self-serving resistance succeeds in making him unsuccessful, it will not be because he lacks the will to lead, it will be said that the people sent him on a mission and did not give him protection from a pack of wide wolves on the corridors of power through the use of their votes. Only Americans can drain the political swamp that today does not want to see America made great again!

Whether these Trump effect leads to America's dooms day eventually or continues on the current state of record breaking economic achievements and boom , it is up to the American people. Divided, America will fall one day. United, they are unstoppable in their quest for a continued universal sovereignty.

Long live the United States of America.

Long live my own country, the Republic of Biafra.